To — My friend on the River. This
marks a years' friendship — has
it been only one year? Julie from Jill

River

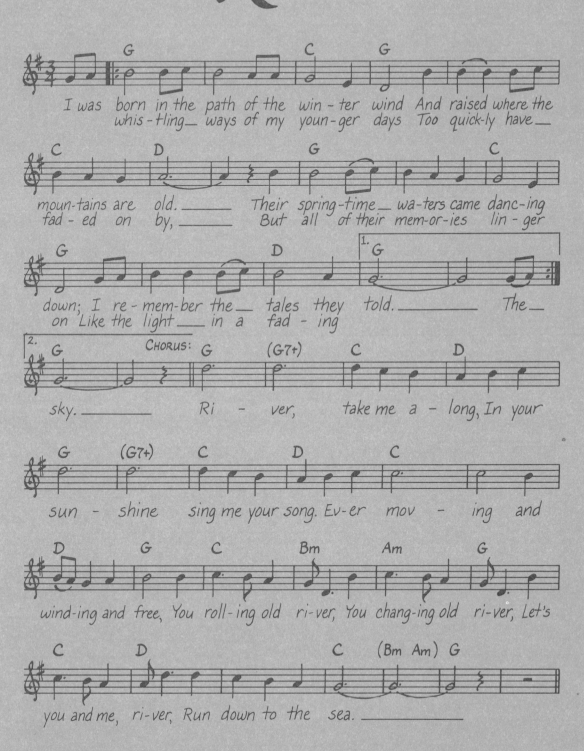

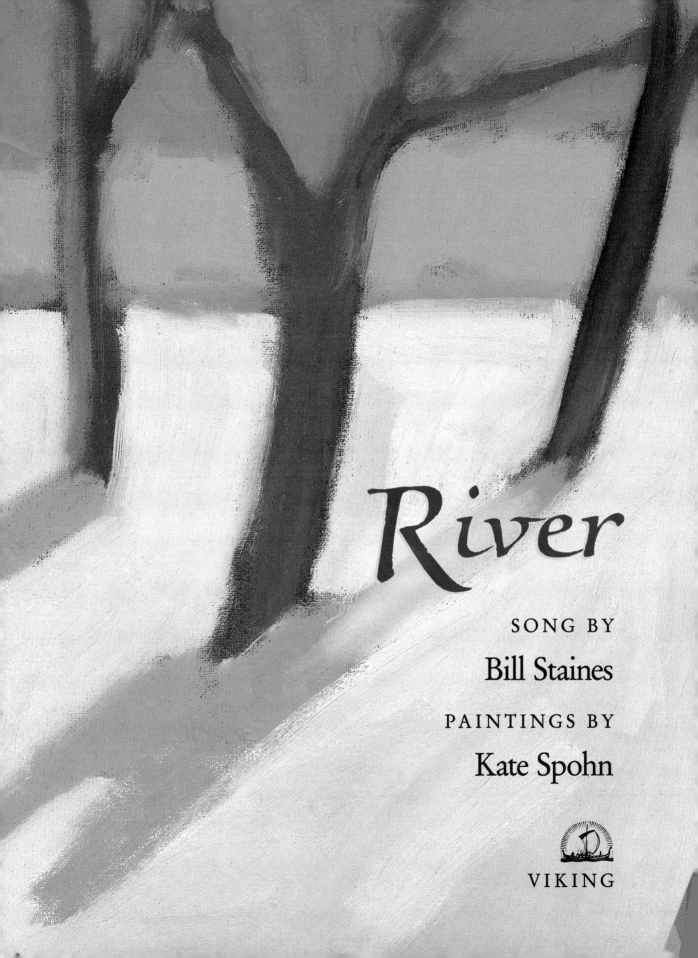

River

SONG BY

Bill Staines

PAINTINGS BY

Kate Spohn

VIKING

I was born in the path of the winter wind
and raised where the mountains are old.

Their springtime waters came dancing down;
I remember the tales they told.

The whistling ways of my younger days
too quickly have faded on by.

But all of their memories linger on
like the light in a fading sky.

River, take me along;
in your sunshine sing me your song.
Ever moving and winding and free,
you rolling old river, you changing old river,
let's you and me, river, run down to the sea.

I've been to the city and back again;
I've been moved by some things that I've learned.

Met a lot of good people,
and I called them friends.
Felt the change when the seasons turned.

I've heard all the songs
that the children sing
and listened to love's melodies;

I've felt my own music within me rise
like the wind in the autumn trees.

River, take me along;
in your sunshine sing me your song.
Ever moving and winding and free,
you rolling old river, you changing old river,
let's you and me, river, run down to the sea!

Someday when the flowers are blooming still,
someday when the grass is still green,

my rolling waters will round the bend
and flow into the open sea.

So here's to the rainbow that followed me here,
and here's to the friends that I know,

And here's to the song that's within me now;
I will sing it where'er I go.

River, take me along;
in your sunshine sing me your song.
Ever moving and winding and free,
you rolling old river, you changing old river,
let's you and me, river, run down to the sea.

To my brother Michael,
and to the Hollenbeck river
where we played as children.

—K. S.

VIKING
Published by the Penguin Group
Penguin Books USA Inc., 375 Hudson Street, New York, New York 10014, U.S.A.
Penguin Books Ltd, 27 Wrights Lane, London W8 5T2, England
Penguin Books Australia Ltd, Ringwood, Victoria, Australia
Penguin Books Canada Ltd, 10 Alcorn Avenue, Toronto, Ontario, Canada M4V 3B2
Penguin Books (N.Z.) Ltd, 182–190 Wairau Road, Auckland 10, New Zealand

Penguin Books Ltd, Registered Offices: Harmondsworth, Middlesex, England

First published in 1994 by Viking, a division of Penguin Books USA Inc.

10 9 8 7 6 5 4 3 2 1

Music and lyrics copyright © Mineral River Music, 1978
Illustrations copyright © Kate Spohn, 1994
Music copyist Christina Davidson
All rights reserved

LIBRARY OF CONGRESS CATALOGING IN PUBLICATION DATA

Staines, Bill.   River / song by Bill Staines ; paintings by Kate Spohn.   p.   cm.
Summary: A young person's reflections on the progress of life are mirrored by the flow of a river.
I S B N 0 - 6 7 0 - 8 5 3 5 3 - 4
1. Children's songs—Texts. [1. Rivers—Songs and music. 2. Songs.]   I. Spohn, Kate, ill.   II. Title.
PZ8.3.S7823Ri 1994 [E]—dc20 93-27864 CIP AC

"River" appeared previously in *If I Were a Word, Then I'd Be a Song:
Songs by Bill Staines.* Copyright © 1980 by Folk-Legacy Records, Inc.
Printed in Singapore   Set in 18 pt. Stempel Garamond